Impressum
Verlag: BABADADA GmbH, Nedderfeld 112 , 22529 Hamburg
Geschäftsführer / Verlagsleitung: Harald Hof
Druck: Books on Demand GmbH, In de Tarpen 42, 22848 Norderstedt

Imprint
Publisher: BABADADA GmbH, Nedderfeld 112 , 22529 Hamburg, Germany
Managing Director / Publishing direction: Harald Hof
Print: Books on Demand GmbH, In de Tarpen 42, 22848 Norderstedt

school
學校

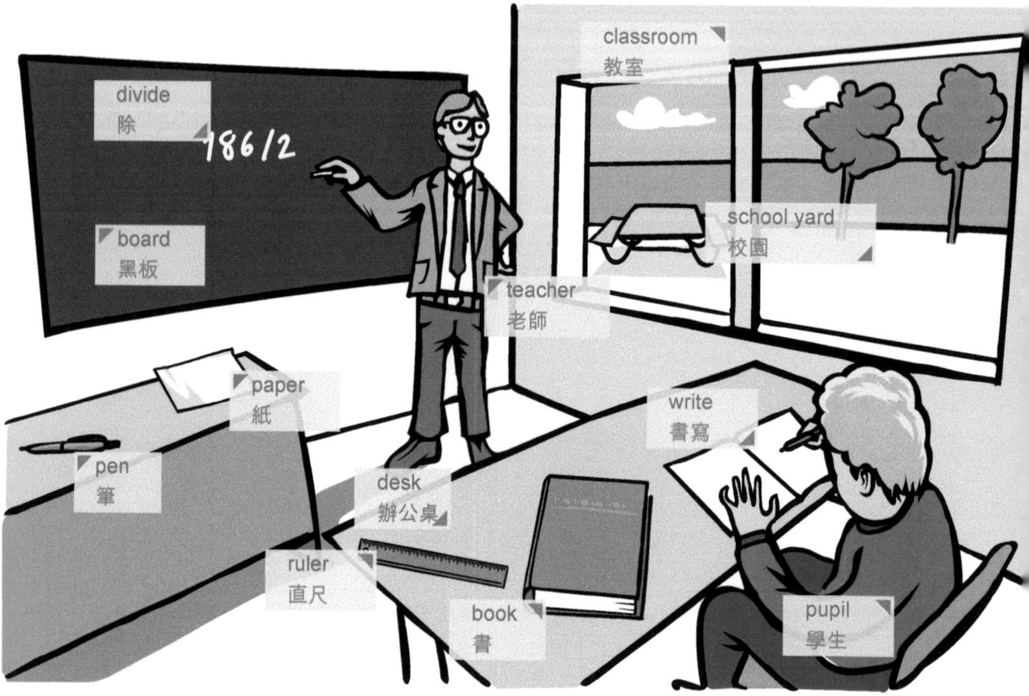
classroom
教室
divide
除
186/2
board
黑板
school yard
校園
teacher
老師
paper
紙
write
書寫
pen
筆
desk
辦公桌
ruler
直尺
book
書
pupil
學生

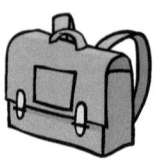

satchel
書包

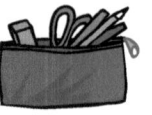

pencil case
鉛筆盒

pencil
鉛筆

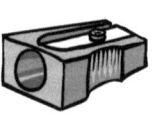

pencil sharpener
削鉛筆機

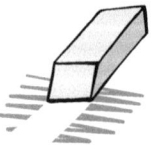

rubber
橡皮擦

drawing pad
畫板

drawing

圖畫

paintbrush

畫筆

paint box

顏料盒

scissors

剪刀

glue

膠水

exercise book

練習冊

homework

家庭作業

number

數字

add

加

subtract

減

multiply

乘

calculate

計算

letter

字母

alphabet

字母表

word

字

text

課文

read

讀

chalk

粉筆

lesson

上課

register

登記

exam

考試

certificate

證書

school uniform

校服

education

教育

encyclopedia

百科全書

university

大學

microscope

顯微鏡

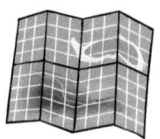

map

地圖

waste-paper basket

廢紙簍

hotel
飯店

Grand

hostel
青年旅社

ROOMS

bureau de change
外幣兌換處

EXCHANGE

car
汽車

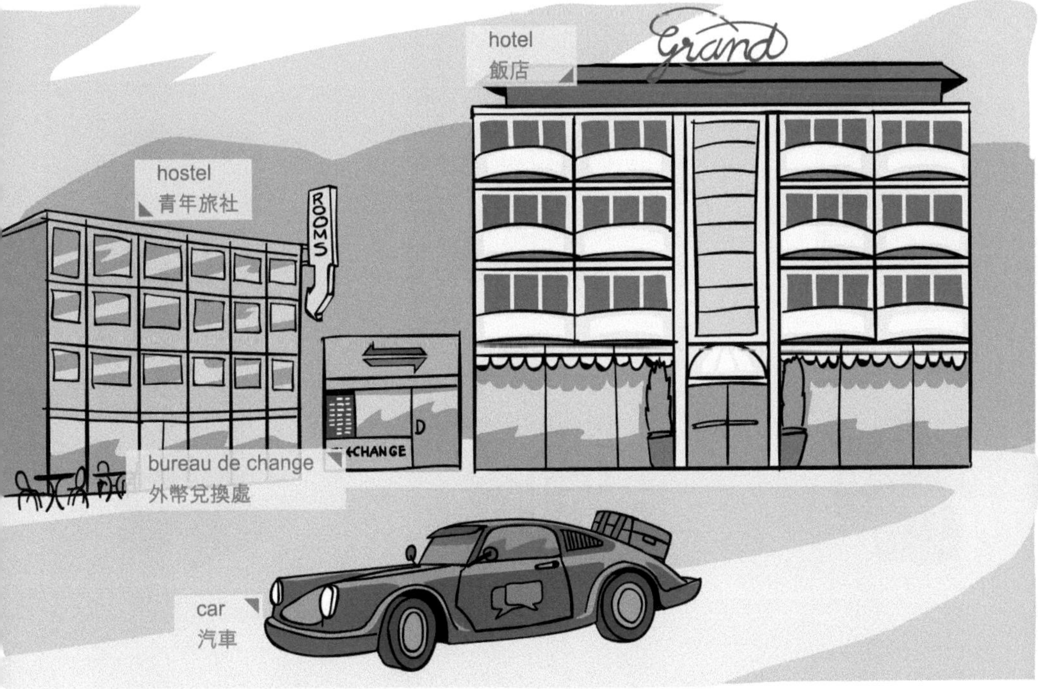

language

語言

yes / no

是/否

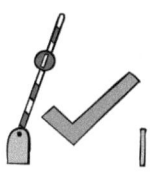

Okay

好的

hello

您好

translator

翻譯人員

Thank you

謝謝

how much is...?

......多少錢？

I do not understand

我不明白

problem

問題

Good evening!

晚上好！

Good morning!

早上好！

Good night!

晚安！

bye bye

再見

direction

方向

luggage

行李

bag

包

backpack

背包

guest

客人

room

房間

sleeping bag

睡袋

tent

帳篷

tourist information

旅行資訊

beach

海灘

credit card

信用卡

breakfast

早餐

lunch

午餐

dinner

晚餐

ticket

票

lift

電梯

stamp

郵票

border

邊界

customs

海關

embassy

大使館

visa

簽證

passport

護照

transport
交通運送

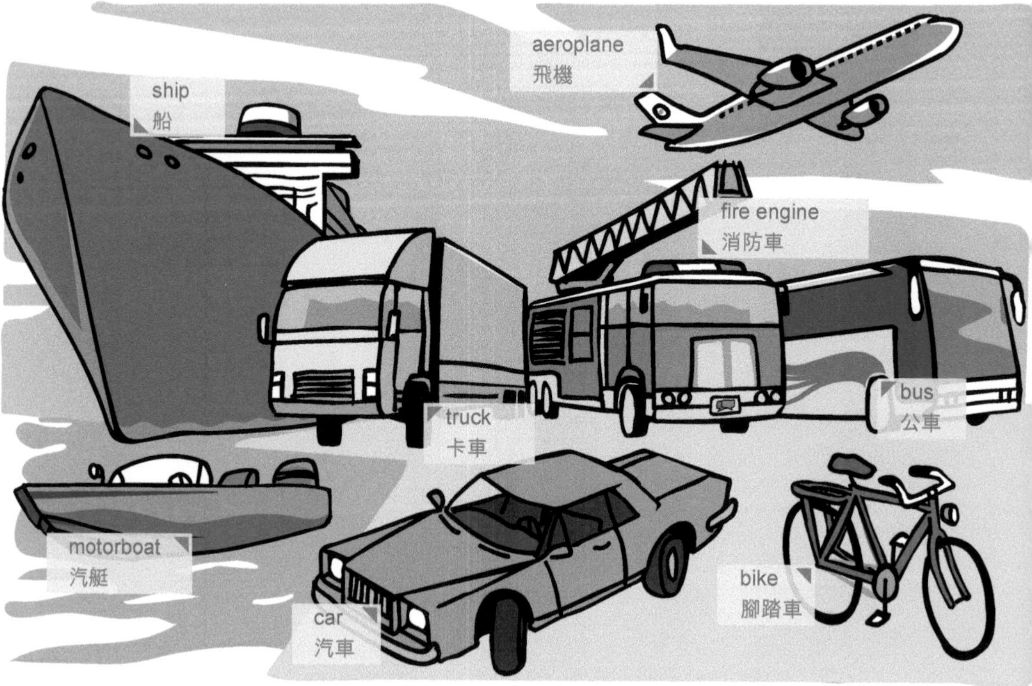
aeroplane
飛機
ship
船
fire engine
消防車
truck
卡車
bus
公車
motorboat
汽艇
bike
腳踏車
car
汽車

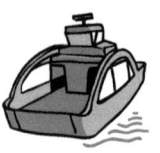

ferry
渡輪

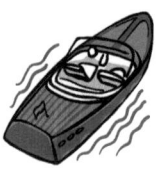

boat
小船

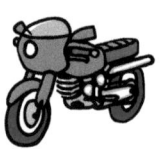

motorbike
機車

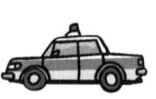

police car
警車

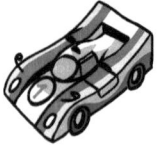

racing car
賽車

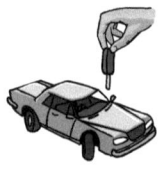

rental car
租車

car sharing

拼車

breakdown truck

拖車

refuse truck

垃圾車

motor

馬達

fuel

汽油

petrol station

加油站

traffic sign

交通標識

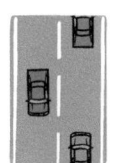

traffic

交通

traffic jam

交通堵塞

car park

停車場

train station

火車站

tracks

軌道

train

火車

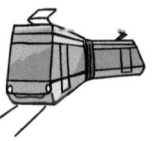

tram

路面電車

carriage

客車廂

helicopter

直升機

airport

機場

tower

塔

passenger

乘客

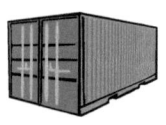

container

集裝箱

carton

紙板箱

cart

手推車

basket

籃子

take off / land

起飛/降落

city

城市

village

村莊

city centre

市中心

house

房子

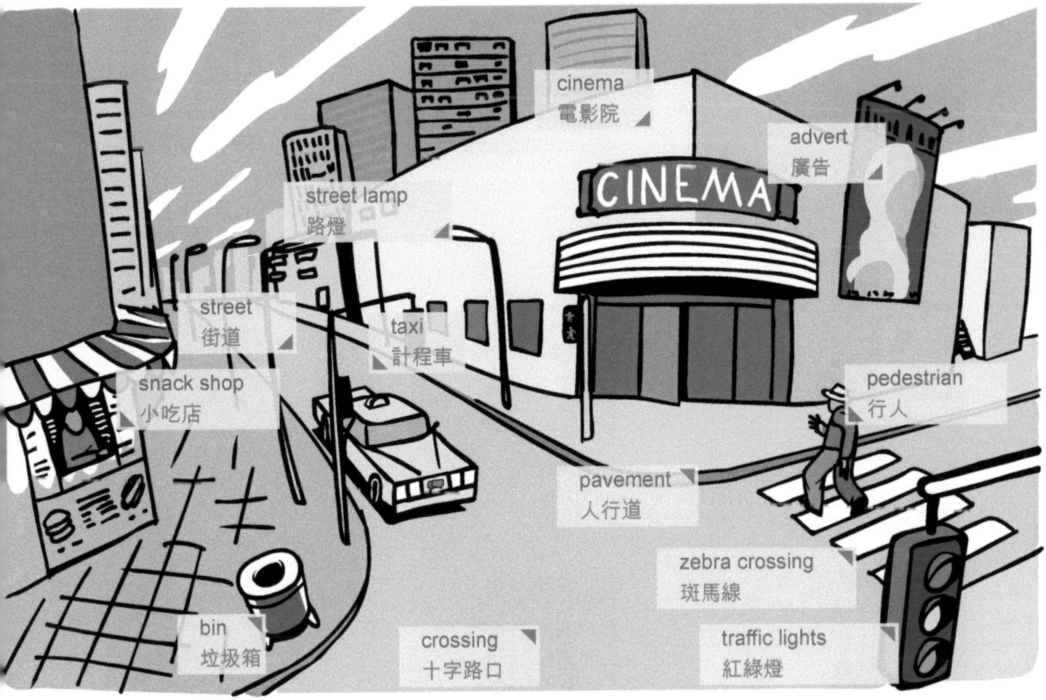
CINEMA
cinema
電影院
advert
廣告
street lamp
路燈
street
街道
taxi
計程車
snack shop
小吃店
pedestrian
行人
pavement
人行道
zebra crossing
斑馬線
bin
垃圾箱
crossing
十字路口
traffic lights
紅綠燈

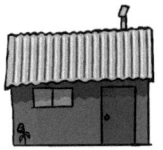

hut

小屋

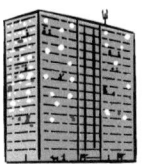

flat

公寓

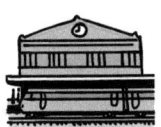

train station

火車站

town hall

市政廳

MUSEUM

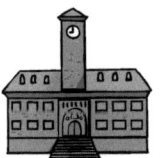

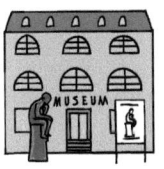

museum

博物館

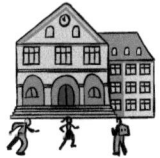

school

學校

university

大學

bank

銀行

hospital

醫院

hotel

飯店

pharmacy

藥房

office

辦公室

book shop

書店

shop

商店

florist's

花店

supermarket

超市

market

市場

department store

百貨商店

fishmonger's

魚店

shopping centre

購物中心

harbour

海港

park

公園

bench

長凳

bridge

橋

stairs

樓梯

underground

捷運

tunnel

隧道

bus stop

公車站

bar

酒吧

restaurant

餐館

postbox

郵筒

street sign

路標

parking meter

停車計時器

zoo

動物園

swimming pool

游泳池

mosque

清真寺

farm
農場

pollution
污染

graveyard
墓地

church
教堂

playground
操場

temple
寺廟

landscape
地形

signpost
指示牌

way
路

meadow
草地

stone
石頭

hiker
徒步旅行者

tree
樹

river
河

grass
草

flower
花

valley

峽谷

hill

丘陵

lake

湖

forest

森林

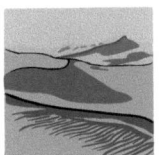

desert

沙漠

volcano

火山

castle

城堡

rainbow

彩虹

mushroom

蘑菇

palm tree

棕櫚樹

mosquito

蚊子

fly

蒼蠅

ant

螞蟻

bee

蜜蜂

spider

蜘蛛

beetle

甲蟲

frog

青蛙

squirrel

松鼠

hedgehog

刺蝟

hare

野兔

owl

貓頭鷹

bird

鳥

swan

天鵝

boar

野豬

deer

鹿

moose

麋鹿

dam

水壩

wind turbine

風力發電機

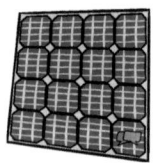

solar panel

太陽能電池板

climate

氣候

restaurant
餐館

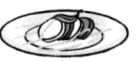

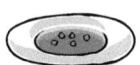

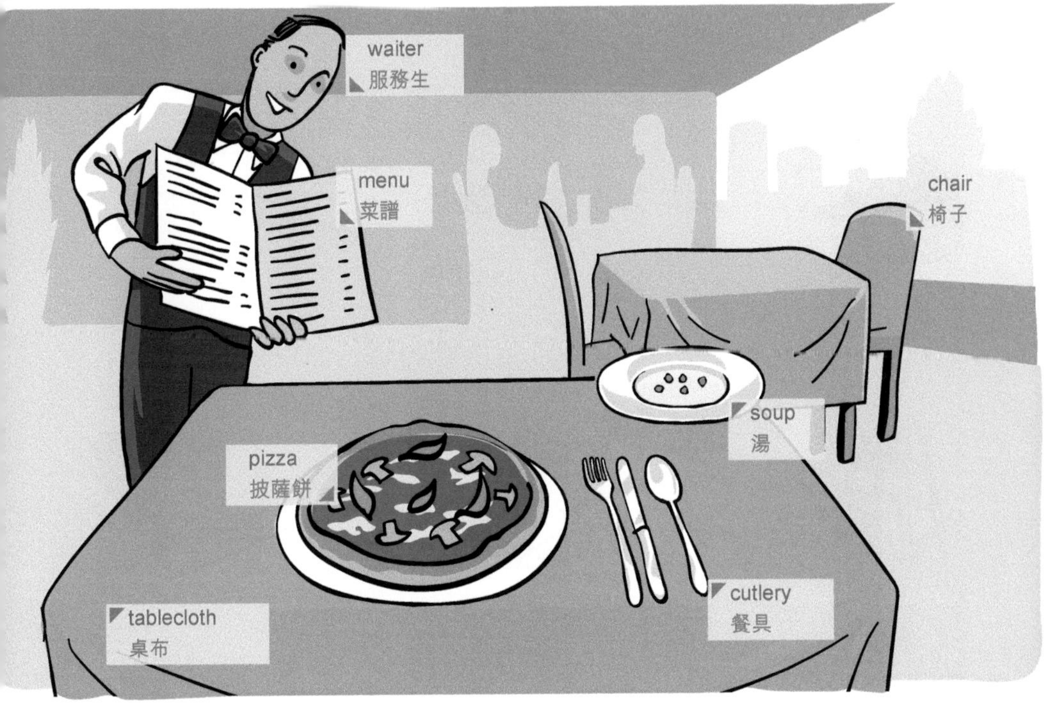
waiter
服務生
menu
菜譜
chair
椅子
soup
湯
pizza
披薩餅
cutlery
餐具
tablecloth
桌布

starter

前菜

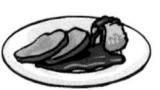

main course

主菜

dessert

甜點

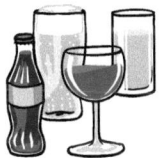

drinks

飲料

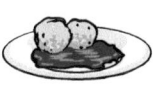

food

食物

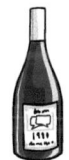

bottle

瓶子

fast food

速食

street food

街邊小吃

teapot

茶壺

sugar bowl

糖盒

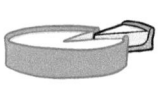

portion

一份飯菜

espresso machine

義式咖啡機

high chair

高腳椅

bill

帳單

tray

托盤

knife

刀

fork

餐叉

spoon

勺子

teaspoon

茶匙

serviette

餐巾

glass

玻璃杯

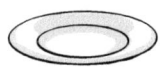

plate

碟子

soup plate

湯盤

saucer

碟子

sauce

醬

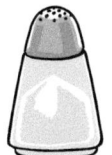

salt pot

鹽瓶

pepper mill

胡椒研磨罐

vinegar

醋

oil

食用油

spices

調味料

ketchup

番茄醬

mustard

芥末

mayonnaise

美乃滋

supermarket

超市

special offer
特價
FOR
customer
顧客
dairy
乳製品
fruit
水果
trolley
購物車

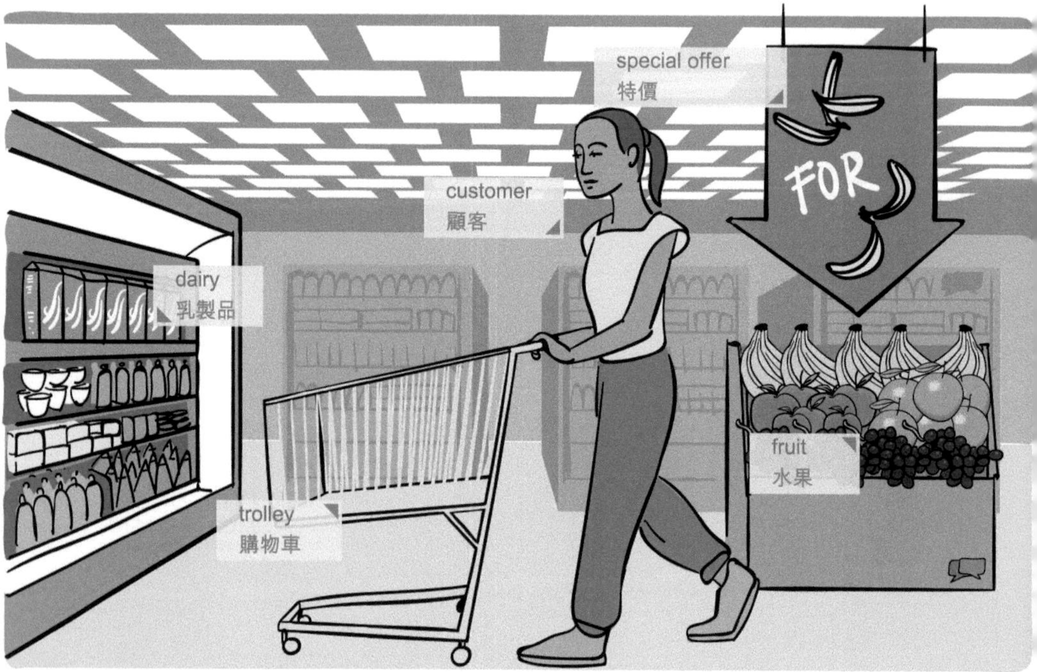

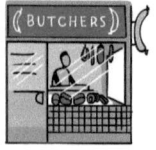

BUTCHERS

butcher´s
肉鋪

BAKERY

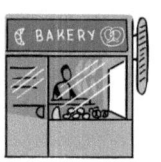

baker´s
麵包店

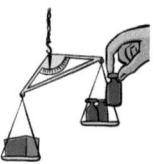

weigh
稱重

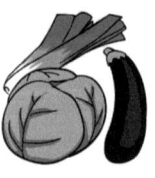

vegetables
蔬菜

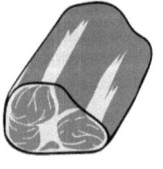

meat
肉

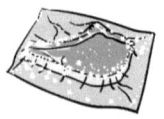

frozen food
冷凍食品

cold meat

冷盤

tinned food

罐頭食品

washing powder

洗衣粉

sweets

甜食

household products

日用品

cleaning products

清潔用品

salesperson

銷售員

till

收銀機

cashier

收銀員

shopping list

購物清單

opening hours

開放時間

wallet

錢包

credit card

信用卡

bag

袋子

plastic bag

塑膠袋

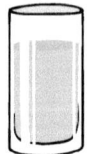

water

水

juice

果汁

milk

牛奶

coke

可樂

wine

紅酒

beer

啤酒

alcohol

酒

cocoa

可可

tea

茶

coffee

咖啡

espresso

義式濃縮咖啡

cappuccino

卡布奇諾

banana

香蕉

apple

蘋果

orange

柳丁

melon

西瓜

lemon

檸檬

carrot

胡蘿蔔

garlic

大蒜

bamboo

竹子

onion

洋蔥

mushroom

蘑菇

nuts

堅果

noodles

麵條

spaghetti

義大利麵

rice

米飯

salad

沙拉

chips

薯條

fried potatoes

炸馬鈴薯

pizza

披薩餅

hamburger

漢堡

sandwich

三明治

cutlet

炸豬排

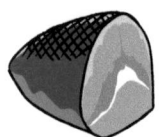

ham

火腿

salami

義大利臘腸

sausage

香腸

chicken

雞肉

roast

烤肉

fish

魚

porridge oats

燕麥片

muesli

木斯里

cornflakes

玉米片

flour

麵粉

croissant

牛角麵包

bread roll

麵包捲

bread

麵包

toast

吐司

biscuits

餅乾

butter

奶油

curd

凝乳

cake

蛋糕

egg

蛋

fried egg

煎蛋

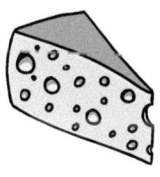

cheese

起司

food - 食物

ice cream

冰淇淋

sugar

糖

honey

蜂蜜

jam

果醬

chocolate spread

巧克力醬

curry

咖哩

goat

山羊

cow

奶牛

calf

小牛

pig

豬

piglet

小豬

bull

公牛

goose

鵝

duck

鴨

chick

小雞

hen

母雞

cock

公雞

rat

鼠

cat

貓

mouse

老鼠

ox

牛

dog

狗

doghouse

狗屋

garden hose

花園澆水軟管

watering can

澆水壺

scythe

長柄大鐮刀

plough

犁

sickle

鐮刀

hoe

鋤頭

pitchfork

長柄草耙

axc

斧頭

wheelbarrow

獨輪手推車

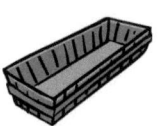

trough

飼料槽

milk can

牛奶罐

sack

麻布袋

fence

柵欄

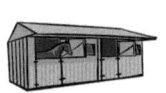

stable

馬廄

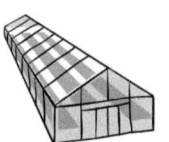

greenhouse

溫室

soil

土壤

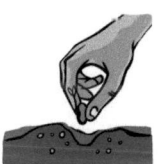

seed

種子

fertilizer

肥料

combine harvester

聯合收割機

harvest

收割

harvest

收割

yams

地瓜

wheat

小麥

soy

大豆

potato

土豆

corn

玉米

rapeseed

油菜籽

fruit tree

果樹

cassava

樹薯

cereals

穀物

house
房子

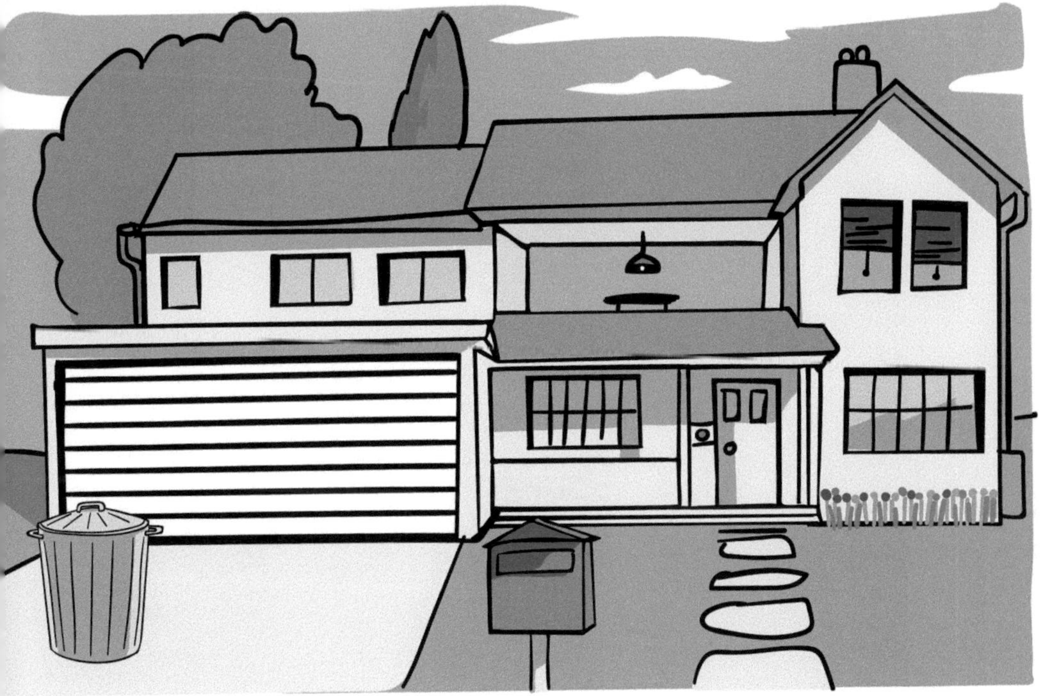

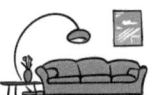

living room

客廳

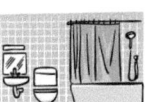

bathroom

浴室

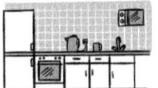

kitchen

廚房

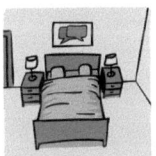

bedroom

臥室

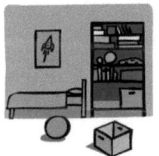

child's room

兒童房

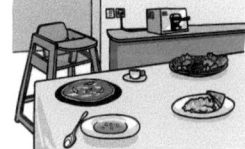

dining room

餐廳

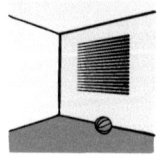

floor

地板

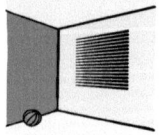

wall

牆壁

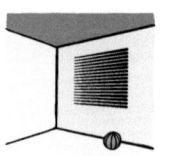

ceiling

天花板

cellar

地窖

sauna

三溫暖

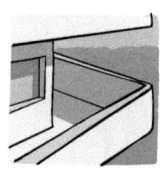

balcony

陽臺

terrace

露臺

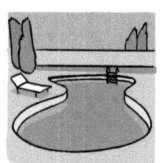

pool

游泳池

lawn mower

割草機

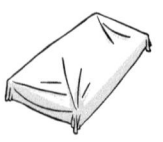

sheet

被單

bedspread

床罩

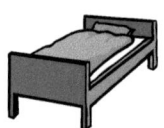

bed

床

broom

掃帚

bucket

水桶

switch

開關

living room
客廳

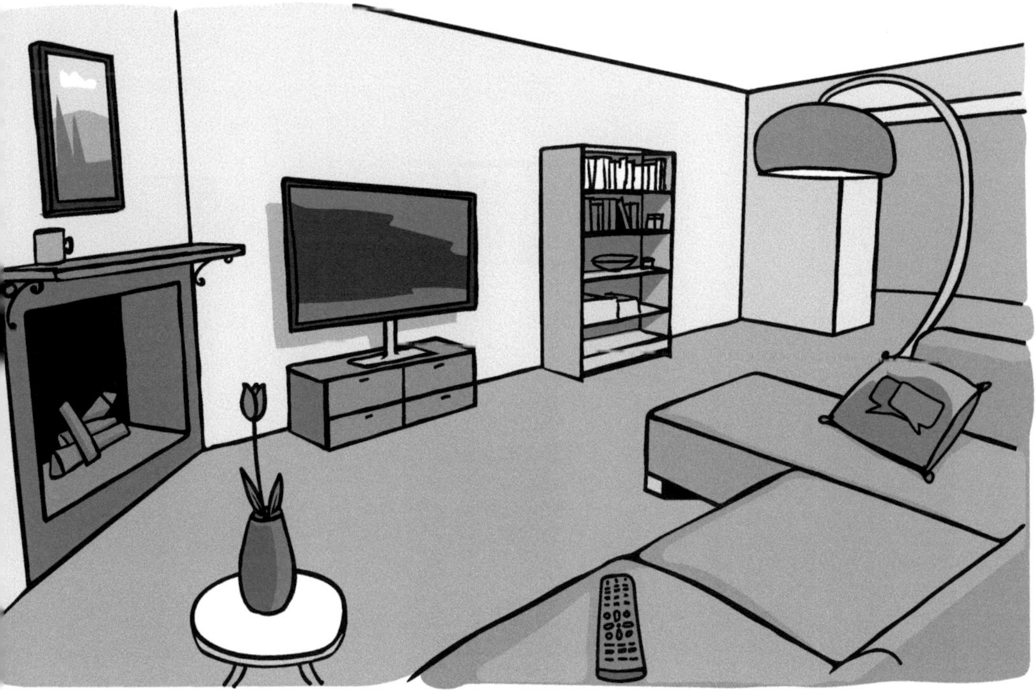

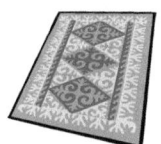

carpet

地毯

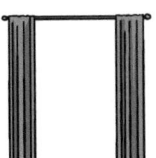

curtain

窗簾

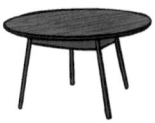

table

餐桌

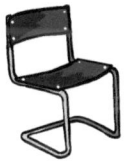

chair

椅子

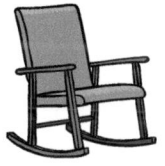

rocking chair

搖椅

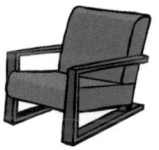

armchair

扶手椅

book

書

blanket

毯子

decoration

裝飾品

firewood

木柴

film

電影

hi-fi equipment

高傳真音響

key

鑰匙

newspaper

報紙

painting

油畫

poster

海報

radio

收音機

notepad

筆記本

hoover

吸塵器

cactus

仙人掌

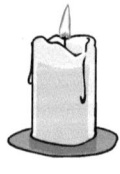

candle

蠟燭

kitchen
廚房

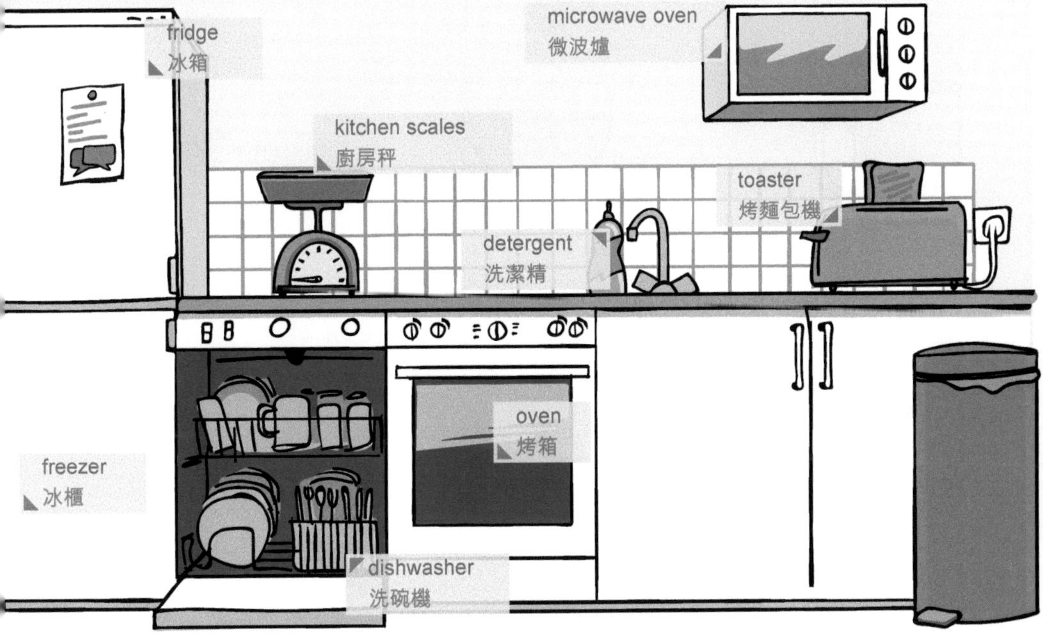
fridge
冰箱
microwave oven
微波爐
kitchen scales
廚房秤
toaster
烤麵包機
detergent
洗潔精
oven
烤箱
freezer
冰櫃
dishwasher
洗碗機

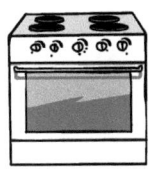

cooker

炊具

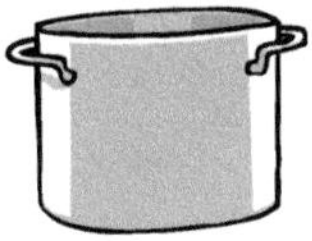

pot

鍋

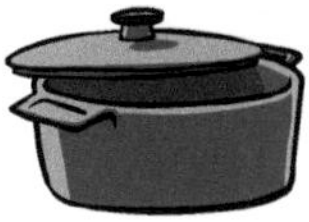

cast-iron pot

鑄鐵鍋

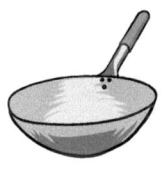

wok / kadai

炒鍋

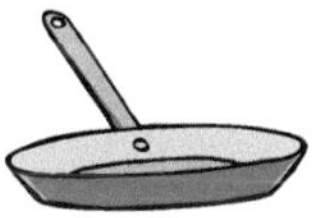

pan

平底鍋

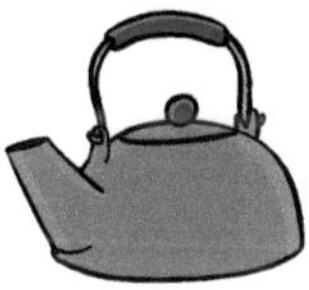

kettle

水壺

steamer

蒸鍋

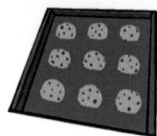

baking tray

烤盤

crockery

陶瓷鍋

mug

馬克杯

bowl

碗

chopsticks

筷子

ladle

長柄勺

spatula

鏟子

whisk

攪拌器

strainer

濾網

sieve

篩子

grater

磨碎機

mortar

研缽

barbecue

燒烤

open fire

明火

chopping board

菜板

rolling pin

擀麵杖

corkscrew

開瓶器

can

罐子

can opener

開罐器

pot holder

隔熱手套

sink

水槽

brush

刷子

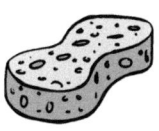

sponge

海綿

blender

攪拌機

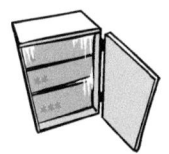

deep freezer

冷藏箱

baby bottle

奶瓶

tap

水龍頭

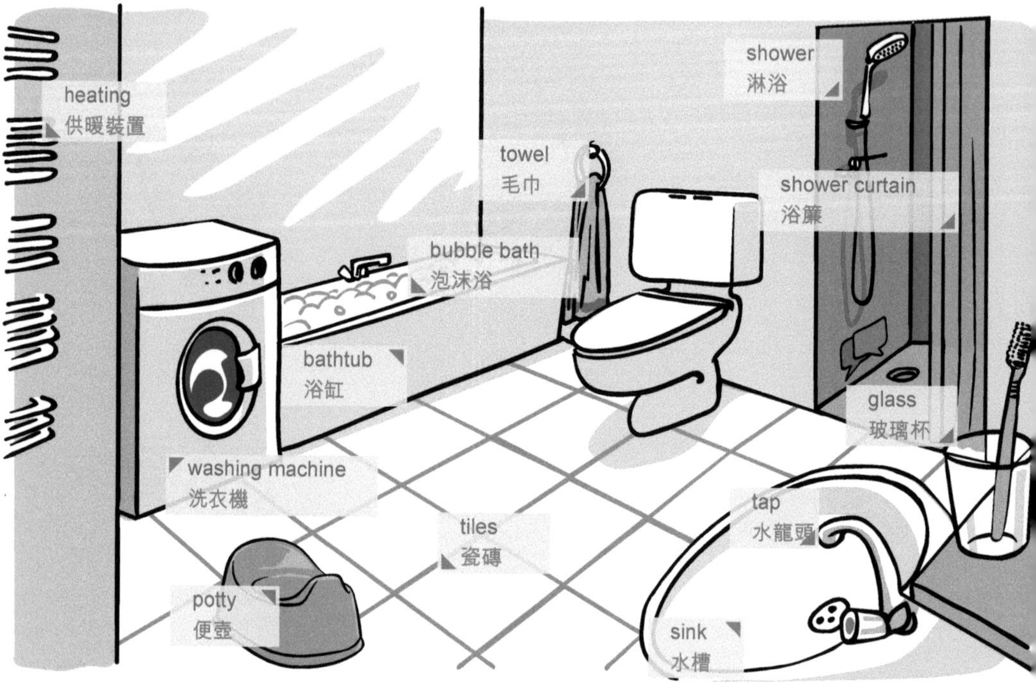

heating
供暖裝置

shower
淋浴

towel
毛巾

shower curtain
浴簾

bubble bath
泡沫浴

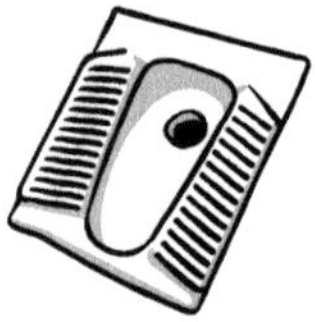

bathtub
浴缸

glass
玻璃杯

washing machine
洗衣機

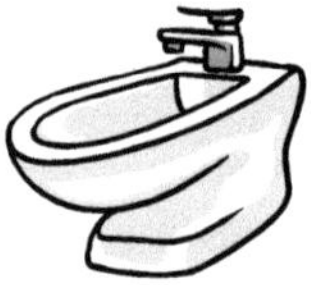

tap
水龍頭

tiles
瓷磚

potty
便壺

sink
水槽

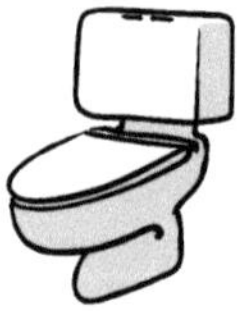

toilet	squat toilet	bidet
廁所	蹲便器	坐浴器

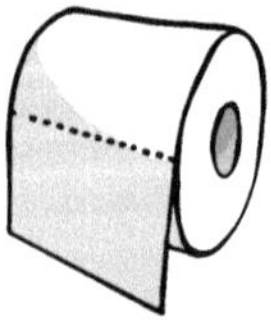

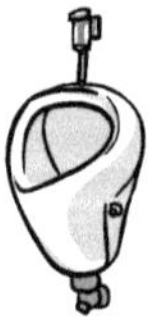 urinal	toilet paper	toilet brush
小便斗	廁紙	馬桶刷

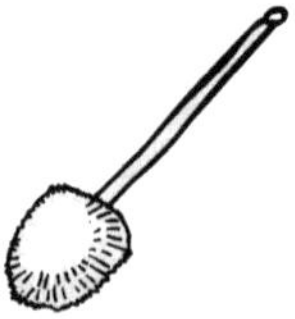

toothbrush

牙刷

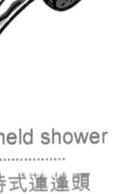

toothpaste

牙膏

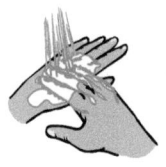

dontal floss

牙線

wash

洗

handheld shower

手持式蓮蓬頭

douche

沖洗器

basin

洗臉盆

back brush

洗背刷

soap

肥皂

shower gel

沐浴露

shampoo

洗髮乳

flannel

法蘭絨

drain

排水

cream

乳霜

deodorant

除臭劑

mirror

鏡子

hand mirror

手鏡

razor

刮鬍刀

shaving foam

刮鬍泡沫

aftershave

鬚後水

comb

梳子

brush

刷子

hair dryer

吹風機

hairspray

噴髮定型劑

makeup

化妝品

lipstick

唇膏

nail varnish

指甲油

cotton wool

化妝棉

nail scissors

指甲剪

perfume

香水

washbag

洗漱包

stool

凳子

weighing scale

計重秤

bathrobe

浴袍

rubber gloves

橡膠手套

tampon

衛生棉條

sanitary towel

衛生棉

chemical toilet

化學廁所

child's room
兒童房

alarm clock
鬧鐘
cuddly toy
毛絨玩具
toy car
玩具車
rattle
撥浪鼓
doll's house
玩具屋
present
禮物

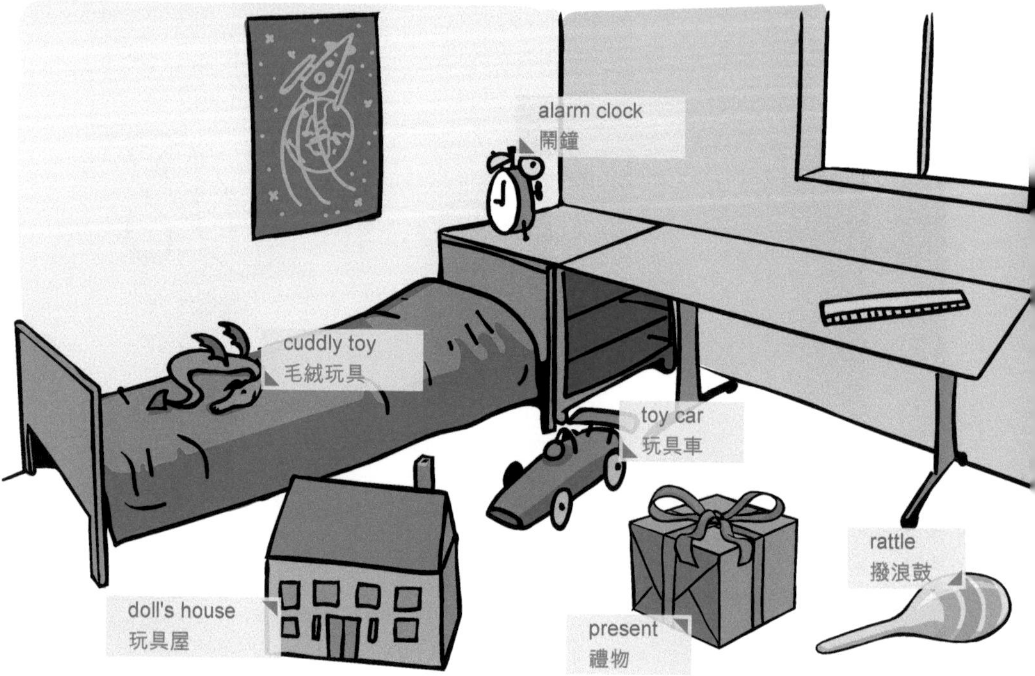

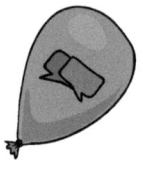

balloon
氣球

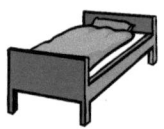

bed
床

pram
嬰兒車

deck of cards
撲克牌

jigsaw
拼圖

SUPER
MEGA

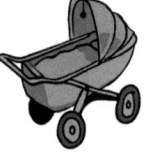

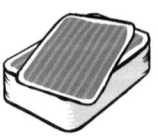

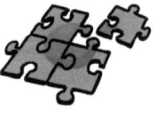

comic
漫畫

lego bricks

樂高積木

building blocks

積木玩具

action figure

公仔

babygrow

嬰兒服

frisbee

飛盤

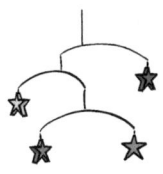

mobile

床鈴玩具

board game

棋盤遊戲

dice

骰子

model train set

火車模型

dummy

安撫奶嘴

party

派對

picture book

繪本

ball

球

doll

洋娃娃

play

玩

sandpit

沙坑

swing

鞦韆

toys

玩具

video game console

電玩遊戲

tricycle

三輪車

teddy bear

泰迪熊

wardrobe

衣櫃

clothing

衣服

socks

襪子

stockings

長襪

tights

緊身褲

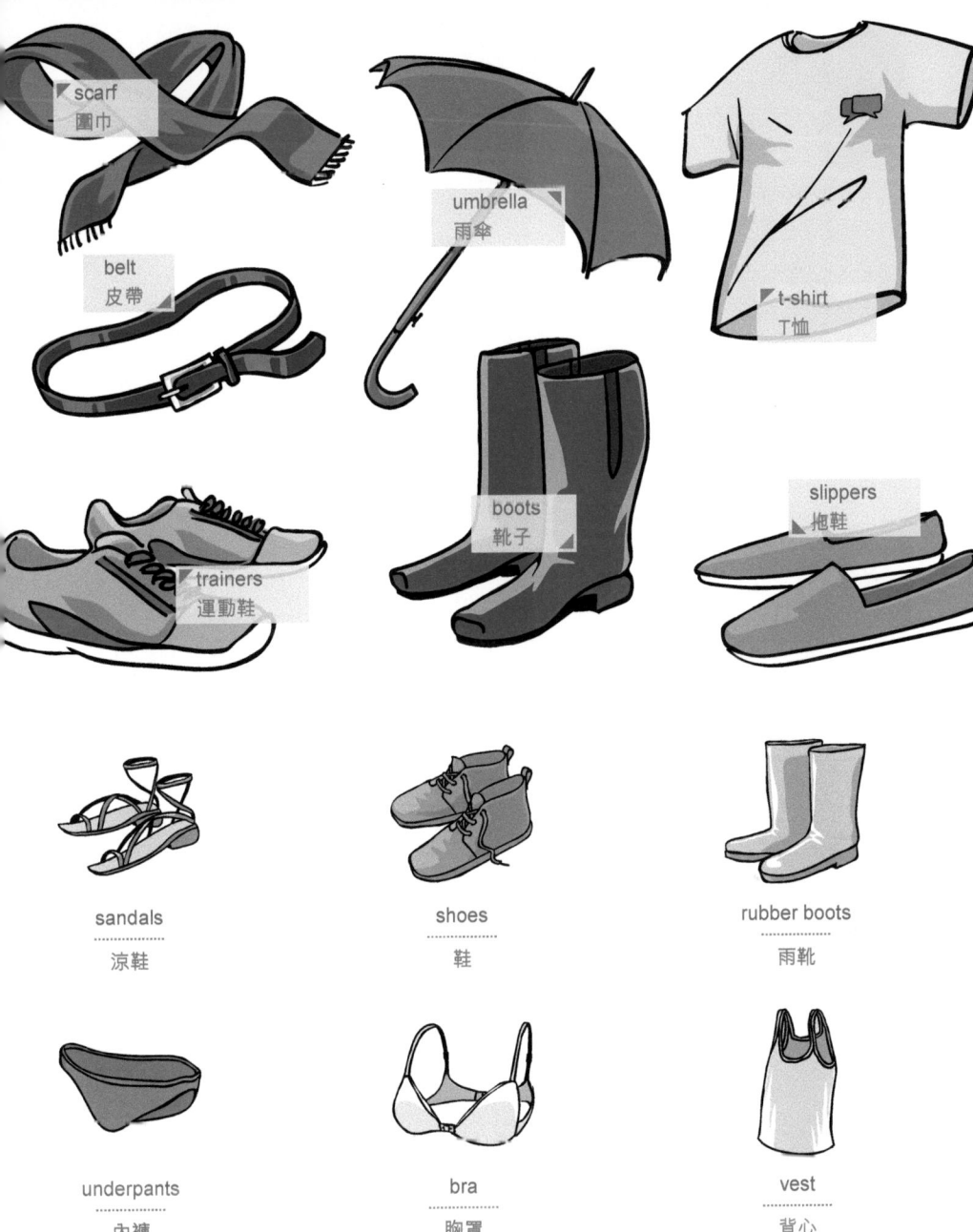

scarf
圍巾

umbrella
雨傘

belt
皮帶

t-shirt
T恤

boots
靴子

slippers
拖鞋

trainers
運動鞋

sandals
....
涼鞋

shoes
....
鞋

rubber boots
....
雨靴

underpants
....
內褲

bra
....
胸罩

vest
....
背心

body

身體

trousers

褲子

jeans

牛仔褲

skirt

短裙

blouse

女式襯衫

shirt

襯衫

pullover

套頭衫

hoodie

連帽上衣

blazer

西裝夾克

jacket

夾克

coat

外套

raincoat

雨衣

costume

套裝

dress

連衣裙

wedding dress

婚紗

suit

西裝

nightgown

睡袍

pyjamas

睡衣

sari

莎麗

headscarf

頭巾

turban

包頭巾

burqa

波卡

kaftan

卡夫坦

abaya

(阿拉伯式)長袍

swimsuit

泳衣

trunks

男式泳褲

shorts

短褲

tracksuit

運動服

apron

圍裙

gloves

手套

button

鈕扣

glasses

眼鏡

bracelet

手鏈

necklace

項鍊

ring

戒指

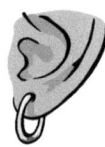

earring

耳環

cap

便帽

coat hanger

衣架

hat

帽子

tie

領帶

zip

拉鍊

helmet

安全帽

braces

背帶

school uniform

校服

uniform

制服

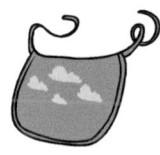

bib

圍兜

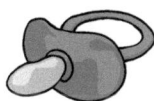

dummy

安撫奶嘴

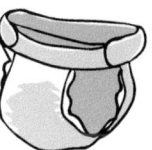

nappy

尿布

office
辦公室

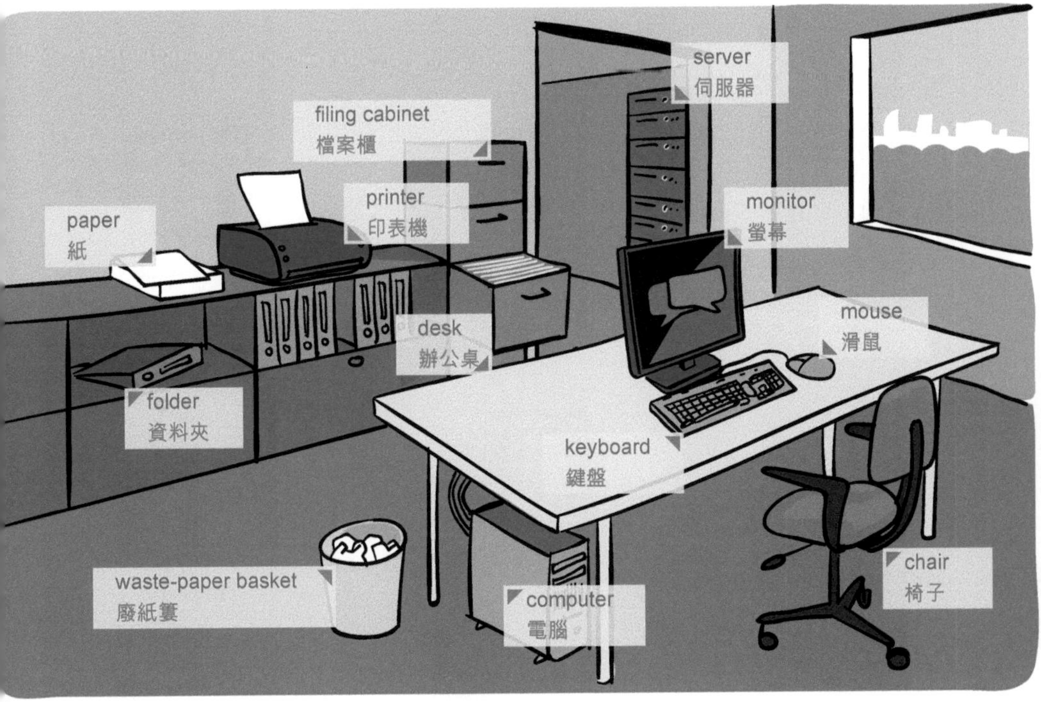
server
伺服器
filing cabinet
檔案櫃
printer
印表機
paper
紙
monitor
螢幕
mouse
滑鼠
desk
辦公桌
folder
資料夾
keyboard
鍵盤
chair
椅子
waste-paper basket
廢紙簍
computer
電腦

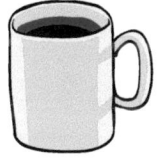

coffee mug

咖啡杯

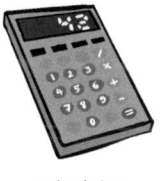

calculator

計算機

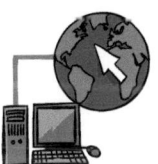

internet

網際網路

laptop

筆記型電腦

letter

信件

message

簡訊

mobile

行動電話

network

網路

photocopier

影印機

software

軟體

telephone

電話

plug socket

插座

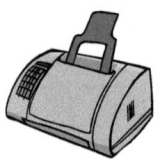

fax machine

傳真機

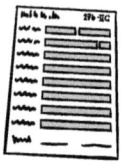

form

表格

document

檔案

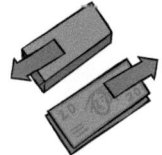

buy

買

pay

付錢

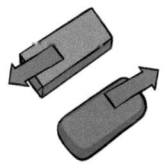

trade

交易

money

現金

dollar

美元

euro

歐元

yen

日元

rouble

盧布

Swiss franc

瑞士法郎

renminbi yuan

人民幣

rupee

盧比

cashpoint

提款處

bureau de change

外幣兌換處

gold

金

silver

銀

oil

石油

energy

能源

price

價格

contract

合約

tax

稅金

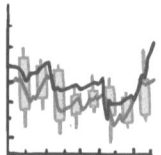

stock

股票

work

工作

employee

職員

employer

老闆

factory

工廠

shop

商店

occupations
職業

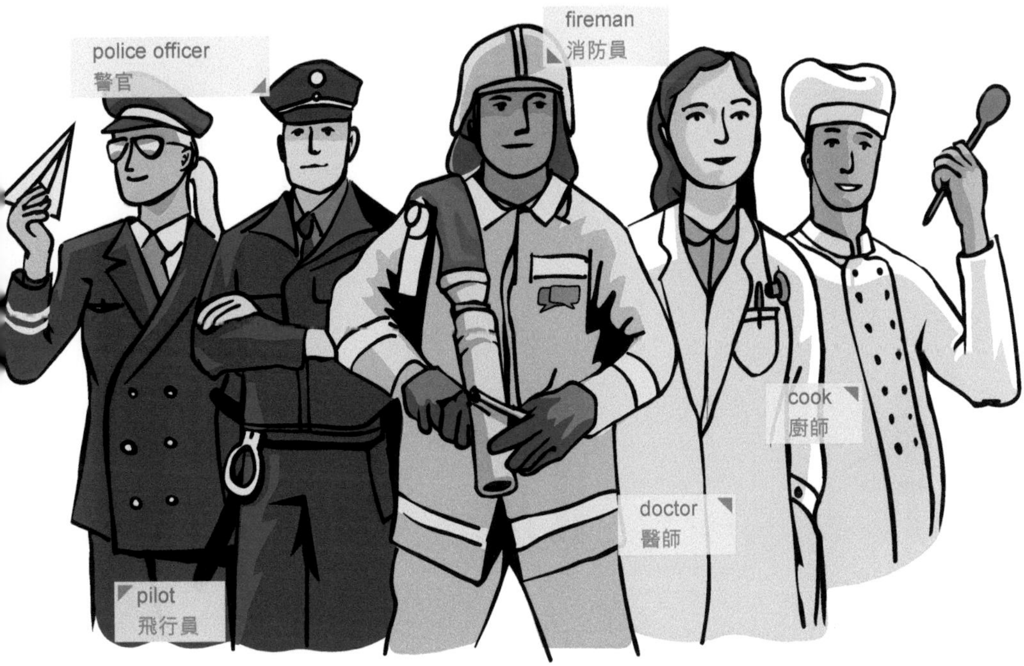
police officer
警官
fireman
消防員
cook
廚師
doctor
醫師
pilot
飛行員

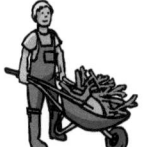

gardener

園丁

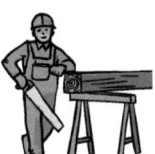

carpenter

木匠

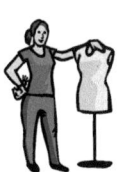

seamstress

裁縫

judge

法官

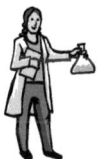

chemist

化學家

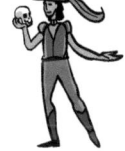

actor

演員

bus driver

公車司機

taxi driver

計程車司機

fisherman

漁夫

cleaning lady

清洗女工

roofer

屋頂工

waiter

服務生

hunter

獵人

painter

畫家

baker

麵包師

electrician

電工

builder

建築工人

engineer

工程師

butcher

屠夫

plumber

水管工

postman

郵差

occupations - 職業

soldier

士兵

architect

建築師

cashier

收銀員

florist

花農

hairdresser

理髮師

conductor

售票員

mechanic

機械技師

captain

船長

dentist

牙醫

scientist

科學家

rabbi

拉比

imam

伊瑪目

monk

和尚

clergyman

牧師

tools

工具

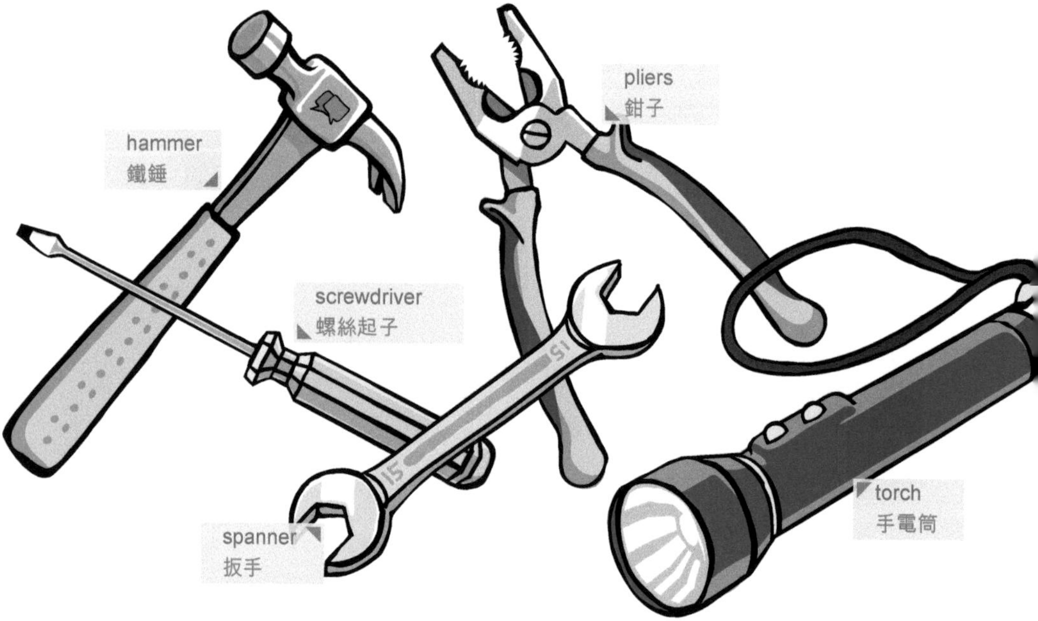

hammer
鐵錘
pliers
鉗子
screwdriver
螺絲起子
spanner
扳手
torch
手電筒

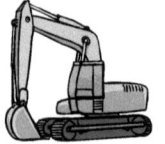

digger

挖掘機

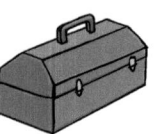

toolbox

工具箱

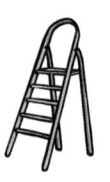

ladder

梯子

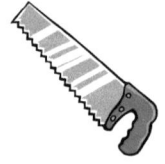

saw

鋸子

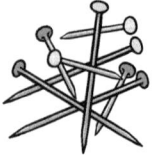

nails

釘子

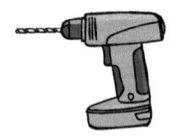

drill

鑽機

repair
修

shovel
鏟子

Damn!
糟糕！

dustpan
畚箕

paint pot
油漆桶

screws
螺絲

musical instruments
樂器

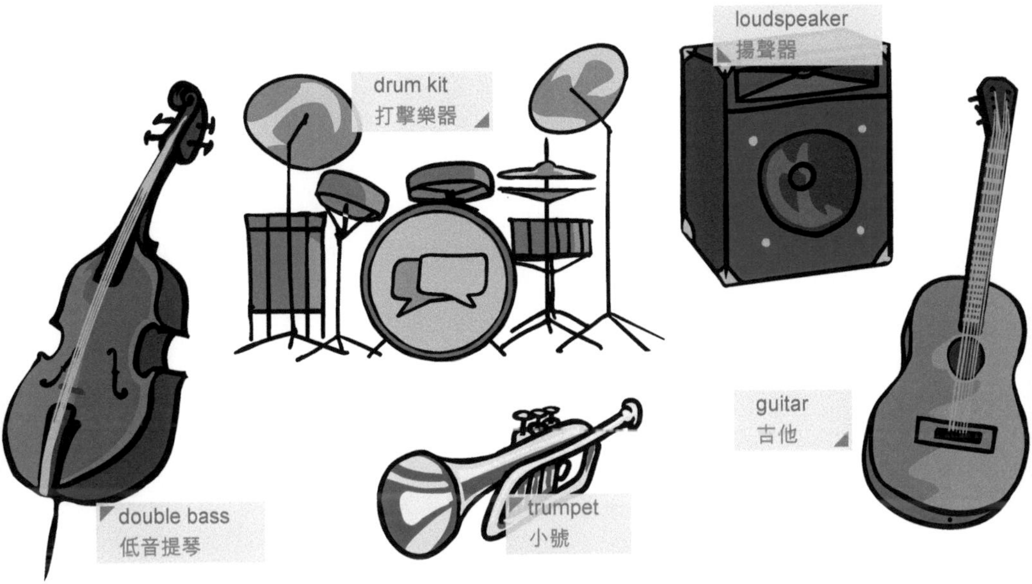

loudspeaker
揚聲器

drum kit
打擊樂器

guitar
古他

double bass
低音提琴

trumpet
小號

piano

鋼琴

violin

小提琴

bass

貝斯

timpani

定音鼓

drums

鼓

keyboard

電子琴

saxophone

薩克斯風

flute

長笛

microphone

麥克風

ZOO
動物園

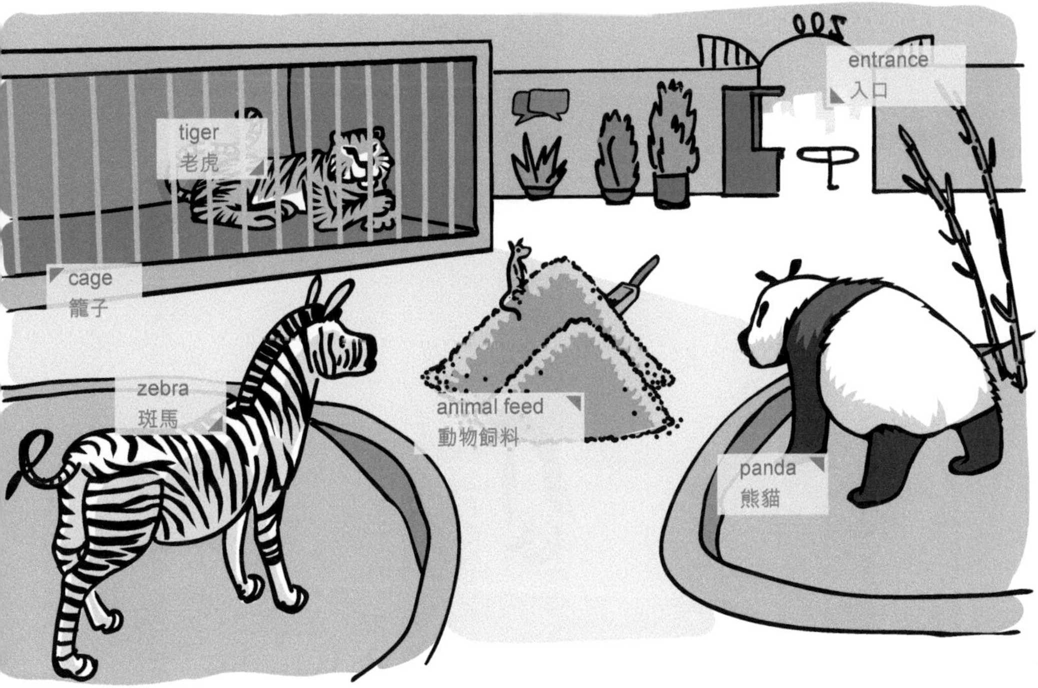
tiger
老虎
entrance
入口
cage
籠子
zebra
斑馬
animal feed
動物飼料
panda
熊貓

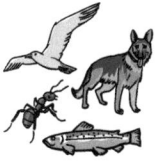

animals

動物

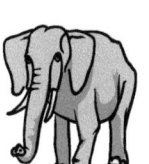

elephant

大象

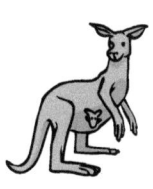

kangaroo

袋鼠

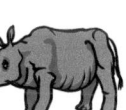

rhino

犀牛

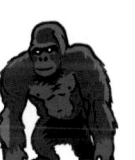

gorilla

大猩猩

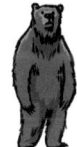

bear

熊

camel

駱駝

ostrich

鴕鳥

lion

獅子

monkey

猴子

flamingo

紅鶴

parrot

鸚鵡

polar bear

北極熊

penguin

企鵝

shark

鯊魚

peacock

孔雀

snake

蛇

crocodile

鱷魚

zookeeper

動物園管理員

seal

海豹

jaguar

美洲豹

zoo - 動物園

pony
矮種馬

leopard
豹

hippo
河馬

giraffe
長頸鹿

eagle
老鷹

boar
野豬

fish
魚

turtle
龜

walrus
海象

fox
狐狸

gazelle
羚羊

American football
橄欖球

cycling
騎腳踏車

tennis
網球

basketball
籃球

swimming
游泳

boxing
拳擊

ice hockey
冰球

football

美式足球

badminton

羽毛球

athletics

田徑

handball

手球

skiing

滑雪

polo

馬球

jump 跳	laugh 笑	walk 走路
hug 擁抱	sing 唱	dream 做夢
pray 祈禱	kiss 親吻	

write
書寫

draw
畫

show
展示

push
推

give
給

take
拿

have

有

do

做

be

當

stand

站

run

跑

pull

拉

throw

丟

fall

摔倒

lie

躺

wait

等待

carry

攜帶

sit

坐

get dressed

穿衣

sleep

睡覺

wake up

醒來

look at
看

cry
哭

stroke
擊

comb
梳頭

talk
交談

understand
明白

ask
問

listen
聽

drink
喝

eat
吃

tidy up
清理

love
愛

cook
做飯

drive
開車

fly
飛

sail

航行

calculate

計算

read

讀

learn

學習

work

工作

marry

結婚

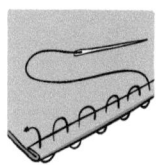

sew

縫

brush teeth

刷牙

kill

殺

smoke

抽菸

send

寄

grandmother
祖母

grandfather
祖父

father
父親

mother
母親

baby
嬰兒

daughter
女兒

son
兒子

guest

客人

aunt

阿姨

uncle

叔叔

brother

兄弟

sister

姐妹

body
身體

forehead
前額
eye
眼睛
shoulder
肩膀
finger
手指
face
臉
chin
下巴
hand
手
leg
腿
breast
乳房
arm
手臂

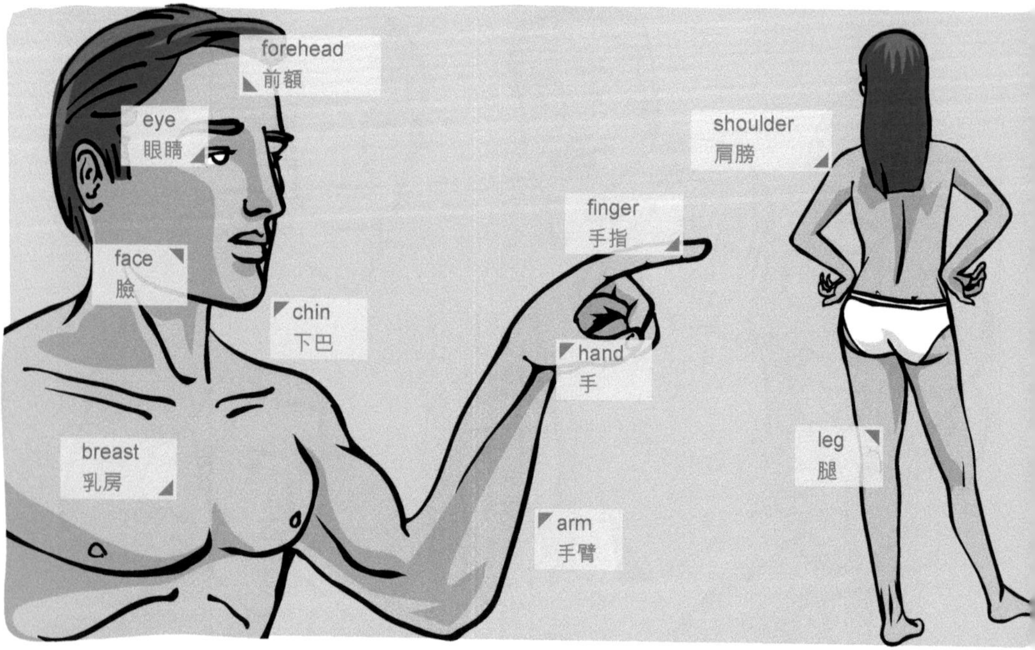

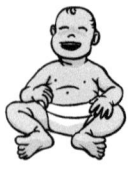

baby
嬰兒

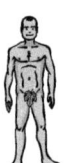

man
男人

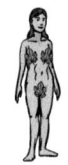

woman
女人

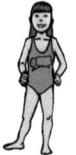

girl
女孩

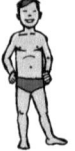

boy
男孩

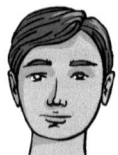

head
頭

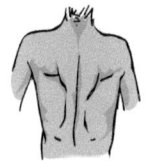

back

背部

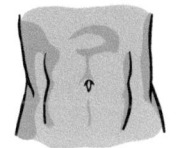

belly

肚子

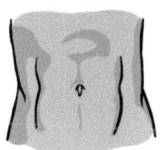

belly button

肚臍

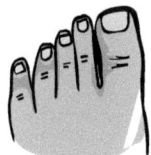

toe

腳趾

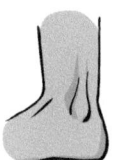

heel

腳後跟

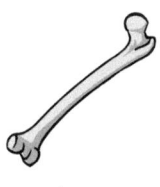

bone

骨頭

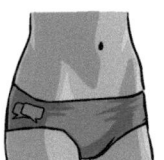

hip

臀部

knee

膝蓋

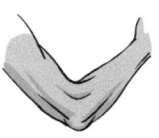

elbow

手肘

nose

鼻子

bottom

屁股

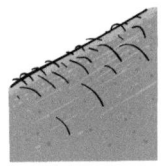

skin

皮膚

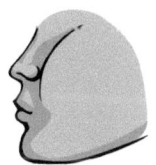

cheek

臉頰

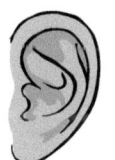

ear

耳朵

lip

嘴唇

body － 身體

mouth

嘴

tooth

牙齒

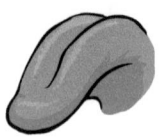

tongue

舌頭

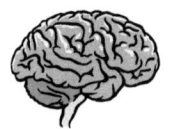

brain

腦

heart

心臟

muscle

肌肉

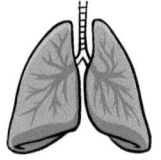

lung

肺

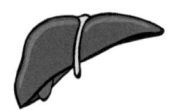

liver

肝臟

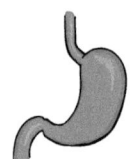

stomach

胃

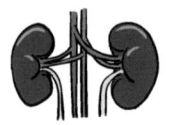

kidneys

腎臟

sex

性交

condom

保險套

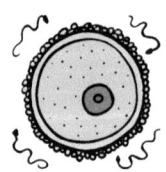

ovum

卵子

semen

精子

pregnancy

懷孕

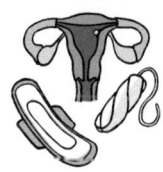

menstruation

月事

vagina

陰道

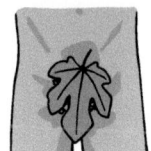

penis

陰莖

eyebrow

眉毛

hair

頭髮

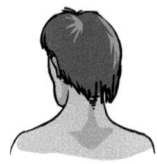

neck

脖子

hospital
醫院

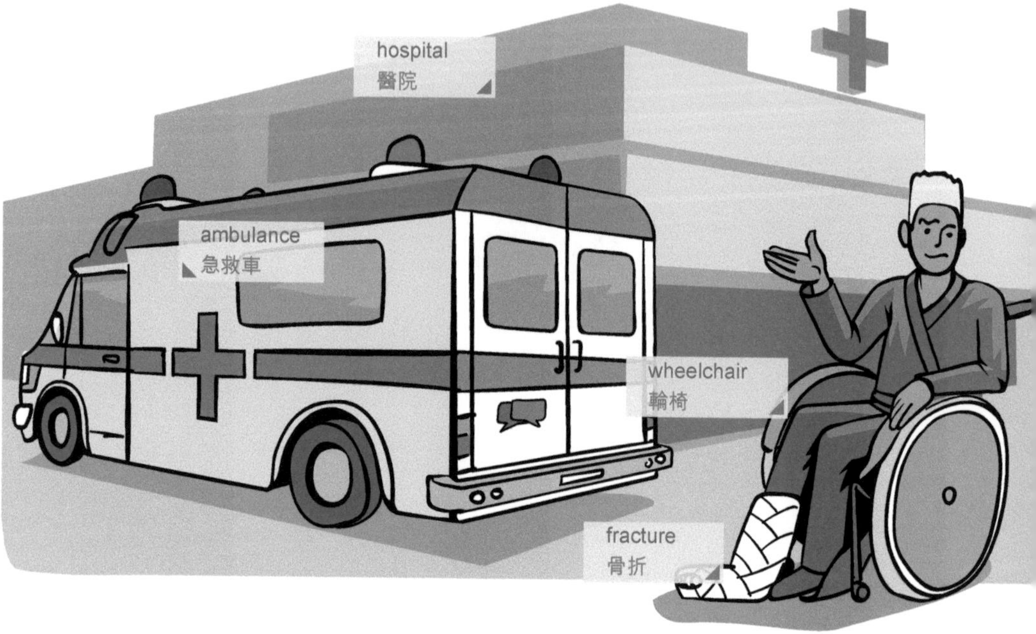

hospital
醫院
ambulance
急救車
wheelchair
輪椅
fracture
骨折

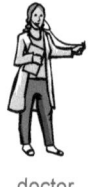

doctor
醫師

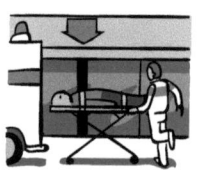

emergency room
急診室

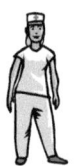

nurse
護理師

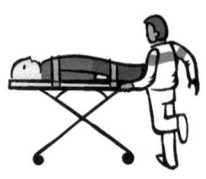

emergency
緊急情形

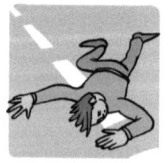

unconscious
昏迷

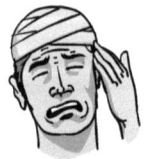

pain
痛

injury

受傷

bleeding

出血

heart attack

心臟病發作

stroke

中風

allergy

過敏

cough

咳嗽

fever

發燒

flu

流感

diarrhoea

腹瀉

headache

頭痛

cancer

癌症

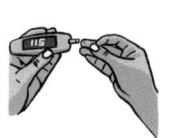

diabetes

糖尿病

surgeon

外科醫師

scalpel

手術刀

operation

手術

hospital - 醫院

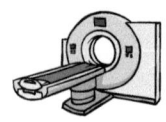

CT

電腦斷層掃描

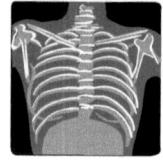

x-ray

X光

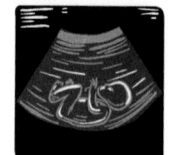

ultrasound

超音波

face mask

口罩

disease

疾病

waiting room

候診室

crutch

拐杖

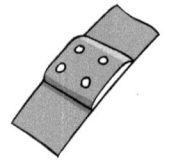

plaster

石膏

bandage

繃帶

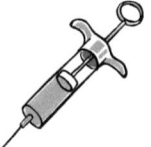

injection

注射

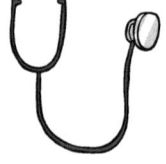

stethoscope

聽診器

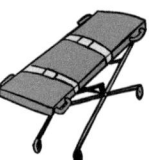

stretcher

擔架

clinical thermometer

體溫計

birth

出生

overweight

超重

hospital - 醫院

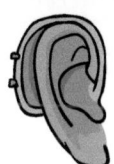

hearing aid

助聽器

disinfectant

消毒液

infection

感染

virus

病毒

HIV / AIDS

愛滋病

medicine

藥物

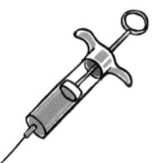

vaccination

接種疫苗

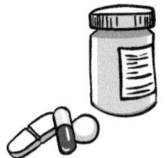

tablets

藥片

pill

藥丸

emergency call

急救電話

blood pressure monitor

血壓計

ill / healthy

生病/健康

Help!

救命！

alarm

警報

assault

突擊

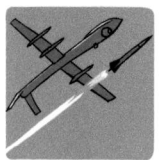

attack

攻擊

danger

危險

emergency exit

緊急出口

Fire!

失火了！

fire extinguisher

滅火器

accident

意外

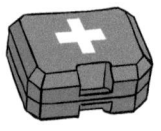

first-aid kit

急救箱

SOS

呼救訊號

police

員警

Europe

歐洲

North America

北美洲

South America

南美洲

Africa

非洲

Asia

亞洲

Australia

澳洲

Atlantic

大西洋

Pacific

太平洋

Indian Ocean

印度洋

Antarctic Ocean

南冰洋

Arctic Ocean

北冰洋

North Pole

北極

South Pole

南極

Antarctica

南極洲

Earth

地球

land

陸地

sea

海

island

島

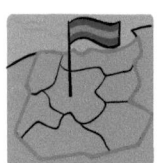

nation

國家

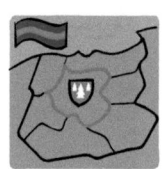

state

州

clock face

錶盤

hour hand

時針

minute hand

分針

second hand

秒針

What time is it?

現在幾點？

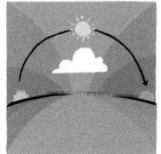

day

天

time

時間

now

現在

digital watch

電子錶

minute

分

hour

時

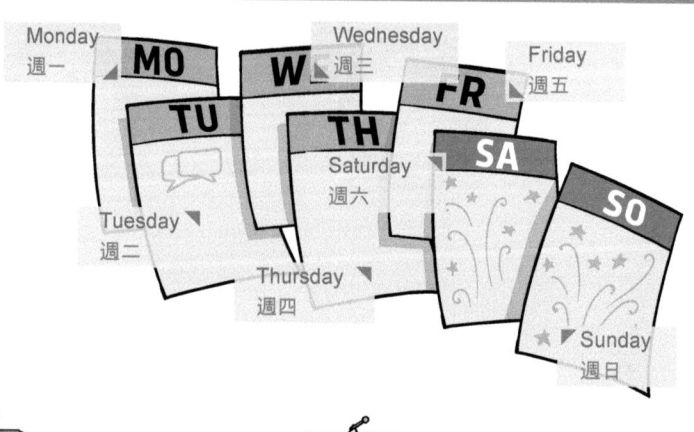

Monday 週一
Wednesday 週三
Friday 週五
Tuesday 週二
Thursday 週四
Saturday 週六
Sunday 週日

yesterday

昨天

today

今天

tomorrow

明天

morning

早晨

noon

中午

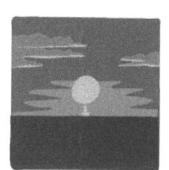

evening

晚上

business days

工作日

weekend

週末

year
年

rain
雨
spring
春
summer
夏
wind
風
autumn
秋
snow
雪
winter
冬

4.APRIL 11°
5.APRIL 4°
6.APRIL 13°
7.APRIL 8°
8.APRIL 10°

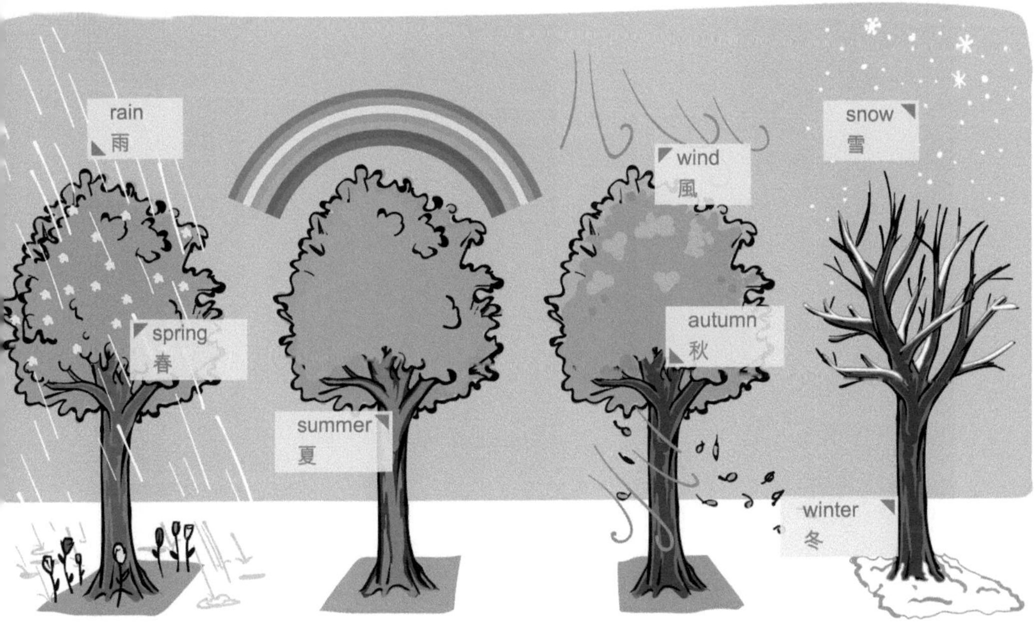

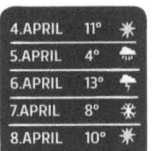

weather forecast

天氣預告

F
C
120
90
60
30
0
-30
40
30
20
10
0
-10
-20

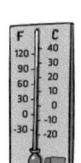

thermometer

溫度計

sunshine

陽光

cloud

雲

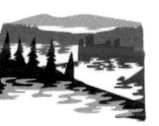

fog

霧

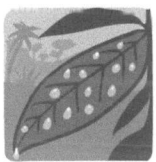

humidity

潮濕

lightning

閃電

thunder

打雷

storm

風暴

hail

冰雹

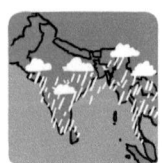

monsoon

季風

flood

洪水

ice

冰

January

一月

February

二月

March

三月

April

四月

May

五月

June

六月

July

七月

August

八月

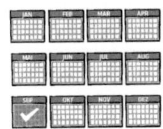

September

九月

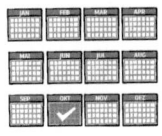

October

十月

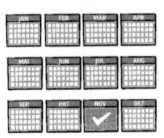

November

十一月

December

十二月

circle

圓形

square

正方形

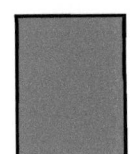

rectangle

長方形

triangle

三角形

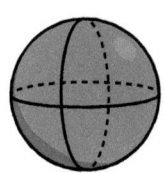

sphere

球體

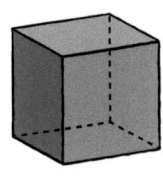

cube

立方體

white
白

yellow
黃

orange
橙

pink
粉

red
紅

purple
紫

blue
藍

green
綠

brown
棕

grey
灰

black
黑

a lot / a little

很多/少許

angry / calm

生氣/平靜

beautiful / ugly

美/醜

beginning / end

首/尾

big / small

大/小

bright / dark

明/暗

brother / sister

兄弟/姐妹

clean / dirty

乾淨/骯髒

complete / incomplete

完整/缺失

day / night

白天/晚上

dead / alive

死/生

wide / narrow

寬/窄

edible / inedible

可食用/非食用

evil / kind

邪惡/善良

excited / bored

興奮/無聊

fat / thin

胖/瘦

first / last

第一/最後

friend / enemy

朋友/敵人

full / empty

滿/空

hard / soft

硬/軟

heavy / light

重/輕

hunger / thirst

餓/渴

ill / healthy

生病/健康

illegal / legal

非法/合法

intelligent / stupid

聰明/愚笨

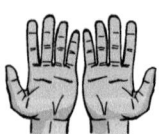

left / right

左/右

near / far

近/遠

new / used

新/舊

nothing / something

沒有/有些

old / young

老/幼

on / off

開/關

open / closed

打開/闔上

quiet / loud

安靜/吵鬧

rich / poor

富/窮

right / wrong

對/錯

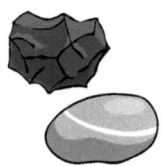

rough / smooth

粗糙/光滑

sad / happy

傷心/高興

short / long

短/長

slow / fast

慢/快

wet / dry

濕/乾

warm / cool

溫暖/涼爽

war / peace

戰爭/和平

opposites - 反義詞

0

zero

零

1

one

一

2

two

二

3

three

三

4

four

四

5

five

五

6

six

六

7

seven

七

8

eight

八

9

nine

九

10

ten

十

11

eleven

十一

12
twelve
十二

13
thirteen
十三

14
fourteen
十四

15
fifteen
十五

16
sixteen
十六

17
seventeen
十七

18
eighteen
十八

19
nineteen
十九

20
twenty
二十

100
hundred
百

1.000
thousand
千

1.000.000
million
百萬

numbers - 數字

languages

語言

English

英語

American English

美式英語

Chinese Mandarin

普通話

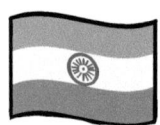

Hindi

印地語

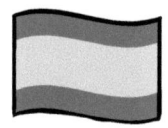

Spanish

西班牙語

French

法語

Arabic

阿拉伯語

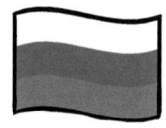

Russian

俄語

Portuguese

葡萄牙語

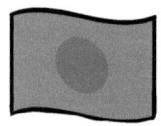

Bengali

孟加拉語

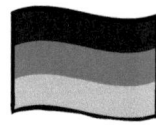

German

德語

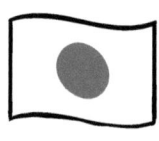

Japanese

日語

I

我

you

你

he / she / it

他/她/它

we

我們

you

你們

they

他們

who?

誰？

what?

什麼？

how?

如何？

where?

何處？

when?

何時？

name

名字

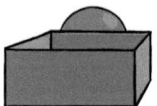

behind

後面

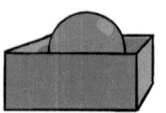

in

裡面

in front of

前面

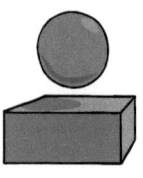

over

上方

on

上面

under

下麵

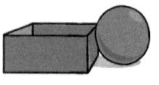

beside

旁邊

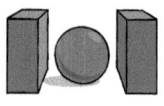

between

中間

place

地點